D0001934

PEOPLE OF WALMART.COM
STATE OF EMERGENCY

A Parody

Adam Kipple   Andrew Kipple   Luke Wherry

 sourcebooks

Copyright © 2015 by Andrew Kipple, Adam Kipple, Luke Wherry
Cover and internal design © 2015 by Sourcebooks, Inc.
Cover design by Lynn Harker/Sourcebooks
Cover images copyright © John Rowley/Thinkstock, Capstoc/Thinkstock
Internal images copyright © puruan/Thinkstock, clipartdotcom/Thinkstock, nidwlw/Thinkstock, AlexanderZam/Thinkstock, calvindexter/Thinkstock, Serban Bogdan/Thinkstock, Mervana/Thinkstock, Nixken/Thinkstock

Sourcebooks and the colophon are registered trademarks of Sourcebooks, Inc.

This publication is designed to provide accurate and authoritative information in regard to the subject matter covered. It is sold with the understanding that the publisher is not engaged in rendering legal, accounting, or other professional service. If legal advice or other expert assistance is required, the services of a competent professional person should be sought. —*From a Declaration of Principles Jointly Adopted by a Committee of the American Bar Association and a Committee of Publishers and Associations*

All brand names and product names used in this book are trademarks, registered trademarks, or trade names of their respective holders. Sourcebooks, Inc., is not associated with any product or vendor in this book.

Published by Sourcebooks, Inc.
P.O. Box 4410, Naperville, Illinois 60567-4410
(630) 961-3900
Fax: (630) 961-2168
www.sourcebooks.com

Library of Congress Cataloging-in-Publication Data

Kipple, Adam.
  People of Walmart : state of emergency : a parody / Adam Kipple, Andrew Kipple, and Luke Wherry.
    pages cm
  Includes bibliographical references.
  (trade : alk. paper) 1. Shopping—United States—Humor. 2. Wal-Mart (Firm)—Humor. 3. American wit and humor, Pictorial.
4. United States—Civilization—21st century—Humor. I. Kipple, Andrew. II. Wherry, Luke. III. Title.
  PN6231.S5467K573 2015
  818'.60208—dc23

                              2014034383

Printed and bound in the United State of America.
WOZ 10 9 8 7 6 5 4 3 2

ACKNOWLEDGMENTS

Who do we even have left to thank by now in our third book? Just kidding! Friends and family have been covered a few times, but we thank you guys as always. Our publishing agent Alison Fargis, our man behind the scenes Brett Fullmer, and our publisher Sourcebooks have all given us their love in these books. We've spent pages upon pages fawning over you guys, our readers and fans, but once again a big *thanks* to you! We wouldn't exist without your support, so we're grateful for it. And there still isn't enough paper in the world for us to properly thank all the people out there that don't look in a mirror before heading to Walmart.

Let's see…who else? Can we thank and acknowledge ourselves? Is that even allowed? Ahhh, let's give it a shot for kicks anyway!

Big shout-out to the authors of this book: Adam Kipple, Andrew Kipple, and Luke Wherry. We are hilarious and creative and borderline average looking. We inspire ourselves every day just by being awesome. If we could grow up to be anyone in the world, we'd still pick being one of the three of us…OK, OK, even we can't get through this whole made-up paragraph without gagging. We're not that great at all, and we certainly don't take ourselves seriously enough to even care. At the end of the day, in this book we truly couldn't have done any of this without our friends, family, supporting cast, and of course you our fans.

DISCLAIMER

We are in *no* way affiliated or associated with Walmart. We also personally have nothing against Walmart. We, along with much of America, shop at Walmart for nearly everything we need. This book and our website are simply satirical social commentary about the extraordinary sights found at America's favorite store. Walmart is Americana, baby!

All photographs and stories have been submitted by the users of the website People of Walmart (www.PeopleofWalmart.com), the rights to which have been granted to ALA Design, LLC. Since we do not take the photographs ourselves, and since many are taken with cell phone cameras, some of the pictures are not of the highest quality and may appear blurry and/or out of focus. So don't look at a picture and think you are losing your sight; it's just somebody's hand shaking excitedly as they run down the aisle with a camera phone.

WARNING: Some of the pictures and stories contained in this book are very graphic. We are not responsible if, after reading a story or looking at a picture, you have the sudden urge to vomit, stab yourself in the eye, stab a nearby coworker or friend, jump out a window, drink bleach, bathe in bleach, clean your eyes with bleach, quit your job and spend the rest of your life in a secluded cave, cut off a limb, or become aroused (really? That's sick!). So pretty much, continue reading at your own risk.

HOW DO YOUR LOCAL WALCREATURES MATCH UP?

Grab your kids, grab your spouse, grab your grandparents and your dog, and take cover; People of Walmart has issued an official state of emergency!

Fortunately for you, all the cases of water, canned food, batteries, flashlights, generators, and other survival necessities are conveniently located at your local Walmart—right next to the back boobs, ass cracks, bottom biscuits, odd animals, ridiculous rides, and all the under-titty sweat you can handle!

After all these years of our fans fighting amongst themselves over who has seen the weirdest thing at Walmart or which region of the country wins the prize for the most Walcreatures, we finally figured that we should open up the battlefield and let each state duke it out in a clash for Walmartian supremacy. It's still undecided if the winner is actually a winner or if the *loser* is the real winner.

So sit back and enjoy the melee as we serve up the top Walcreatures found in each state (and even some international locations—can't leave out our brethren abroad), fill you with some of the most bizarre and useless state facts around, and count down to the best (worst?) Walcreature states! Will your state have enough of the ridiculous to top our ranking? It's time to find out!

ALABAMA

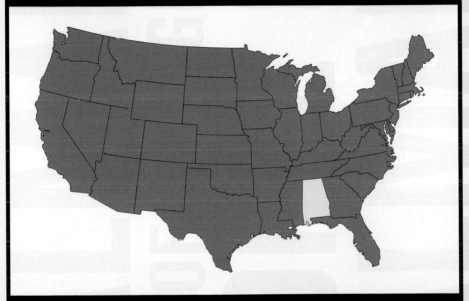

 POPULATION: 4,833,722

 SUPERCENTERS: 94

 IT'S AGAINST THE LAW TO... Flick a booger into the wind.

HELP WANTED

We are now accepting applications for someone to replace the member of our PoWM team in charge of reviewing photos. He looked at this picture without warning and immediately jumped out a window.

I woke up today completely pissed off that it was Monday. Yes, I had a case of the Mondays, and I was miserable. So for all you people who, for some reason, like school or work and woke up in good spirits this morning, this should ruin that and bring you back down with the rest of us.

LOOK AT 'EM DANGLE

It takes a lot to distract me from a blue velvet jumpsuit, but Freddy Krueger's girlfriend here manages to pull off that tough task.

ALABAMA

THAT'S CRACKTASTIC!

At first I mistook these for back boobs, but upon further inspection, that hairy crack has brought me to my conclusion that it is, instead, an upper-back booty. Final answer.

ALASKA

 POPULATION: 735,132

 SUPERCENTERS: 8

 IT'S AGAINST THE LAW TO... Push a live moose out of a moving airplane.

NUMBER ONE GRANDPA

I wonder if his coffee mug says "Number One Grandpa Titties." (Look closely and you'll see what I mean.) If it doesn't, his grandkids are slacking.

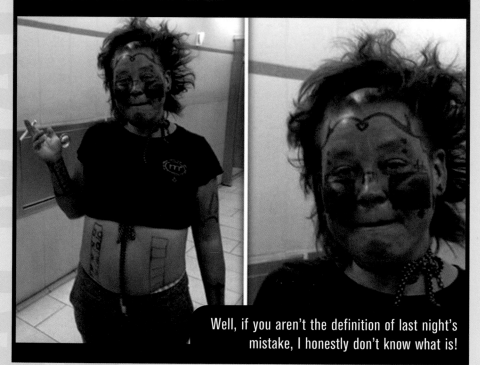

MISTAKES WILL BE MADE

Well, if you aren't the definition of last night's mistake, I honestly don't know what is!

ARIZONA

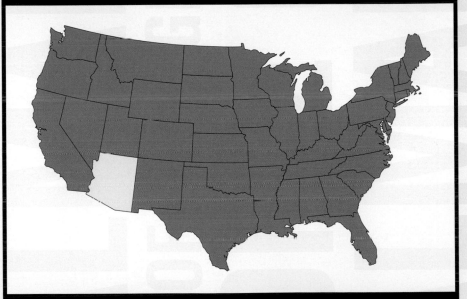

 POPULATION: 6,626,624

 SUPERCENTERS: 79

 IT'S AGAINST THE LAW TO... Have two dildos in one house or hunt camels.

YOU AIN'T GOT NO ALIBI!

Well, if the Dallas Cowboys want to call themselves "America's Team," they need to have a true American cheerleader. I think we have found her.

At least your purple sandals fit. Not really gonna stop my kid's nightmares, but it's a start.

YOU GOT A PURDY MOUTH

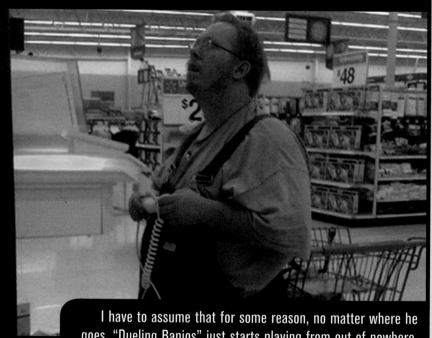

I have to assume that for some reason, no matter where he goes, "Dueling Banjos" just starts playing from out of nowhere.

ARIZONA

RICH IN NUTRIENTS

Does this taste like gasoline to you? Eh, f*** it.

ARKANSAS

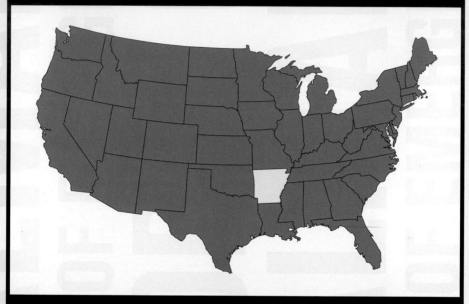

 POPULATION: 2,959,373

 SUPERCENTERS: 76

 IT'S AGAINST THE LAW TO...Keep an alligator in a bathtub.

GIRLS IN YOGA PANTS

I can't decide which is more disgusting. I would probably have to give the slight edge to Miss Flaming Lips on the right.

SWIPE HERE

Who wants to reach in and claim their prize from that Crack(er Jack) box?

ARKANSAS

DIAPER DANDY

I honestly don't even know where to begin with this. We all know my stance on dogs in Walmart, and I'm not a huge fan of dressing up animals either, but I typically keep my cool. However, when we start putting diapers on dogs so we don't have to clean up their shit, that is exactly the point at which I lose my shit.

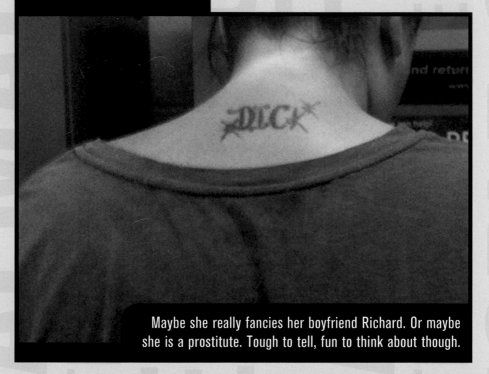

THAT RICHARD IS A...

Maybe she really fancies her boyfriend Richard. Or maybe she is a prostitute. Tough to tell, fun to think about though.

CALIFORNIA

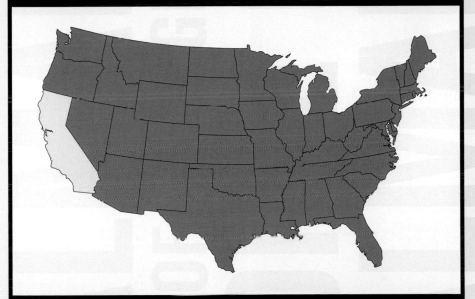

 POPULATION: 38,332,521

 SUPERCENTERS: 120

 IT'S AGAINST THE LAW TO... Go bowling on any sidewalk.

GLASS NOODLES ARE DELICIOUS

It's not every day you see the Rob Zombie—girlfriend look, but when you do it's always special.

20

CALIFORNIA

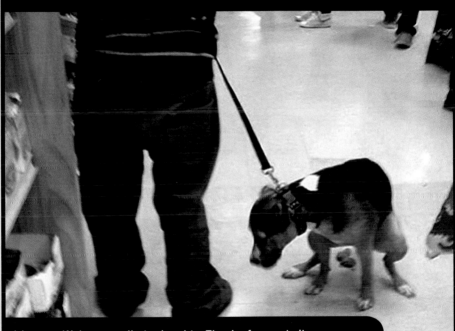

I DID IT ALL FOR THE DOOKIE

It's true, Walmart really is the shit. Thanks for reminding us, pup.

BUBBLES, BLOSSOM, AND BUTTERCUP

I'm sorry. You have a little girl's cartoon tattooed on your arm, bro. You can't come back from that.

DRIVING MISS DAISY

I'd like to come up with a witty caption here, but I'm literally choking on all this loneliness.

COLORADO

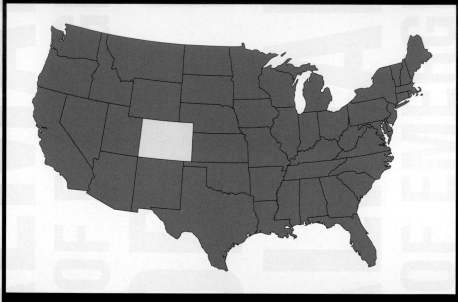

 POPULATION: 5,268,367

 SUPERCENTERS: 68

 IT'S AGAINST THE LAW TO... Ride a horse while under the influence.

A NATURAL BIRTH

There is something wrong with this picture but
I just can't seem to put my finger on it...

WHO'S TO BLAME?

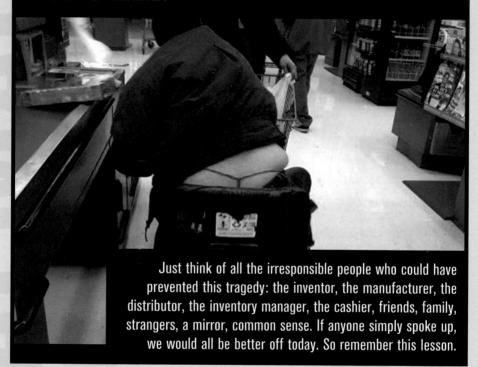

Just think of all the irresponsible people who could have prevented this tragedy: the inventor, the manufacturer, the distributor, the inventory manager, the cashier, friends, family, strangers, a mirror, common sense. If anyone simply spoke up, we would all be better off today. So remember this lesson.

THE DIAPER BANDIT

Hey, hey, look me in the eyes and tell me the truth; I won't judge. Did you use an oversize diaper bag as an actual diaper? You did? Well, I lied. I am judging quite a bit.

GREATEST SKULLET EVER

If I had a biker gang, this chick and her skullet would get an automatic membership. Just picture her cruising down the road on her hog with the wind blowing through her skullet hair. Pure glory!

CONNECTICUT

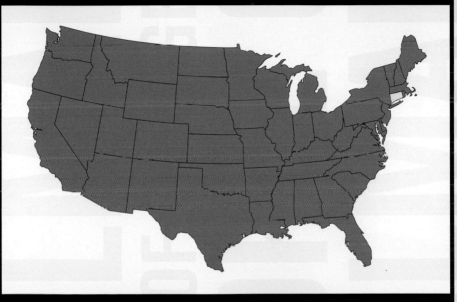

 POPULATION: 3,596,080

 SUPERCENTERS: 12

 IT'S AGAINST THE LAW TO... Cross the street walking on your hands in Hartford.

IN MY WIFE BEAT

I think he's wearing a onesie...like a gangster leotard.

30

CONNECTICUT

RAINBOW 'FRO

Oh, George Clinton would be so proud.

DELAWARE

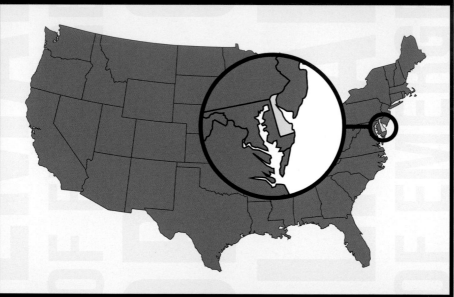

 POPULATION: 925,749

 SUPERCENTERS: 6

 IT'S AGAINST THE LAW TO...Leave your dog's poop on the ground in South Bethany. All persons must carry a bag or risk a $100 fine.

FOZZIE BEAR

Wocka, wocka, wocka! Time to bear down for winter, Kermit.

THE UNDERWEAR BANDIT

It's only fitting that you have your jailhouse stripes on, because you just robbed everyone of their innocence.

DISTRICT OF COLUMBIA

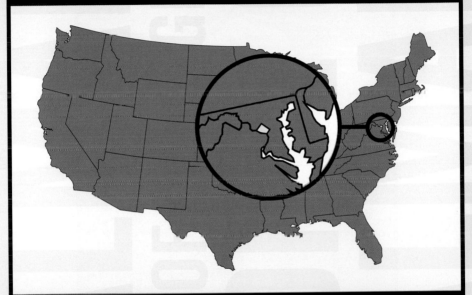

 POPULATION: 646,449

 SUPERCENTERS: 2

 IT'S AGAINST THE LAW TO…Use Santa Claus to sell alcohol.

SWEET UNDIES

Who would have thought the fanny pack would be the *second* most embarrassing thing in this picture?

NOT BY THE HAIR OF MY CHINNY-CHIN-CHIN

I've just decided to start a new website called AwesomePinkSweatpants.com because I can literally stare at those all day.

FLORIDA

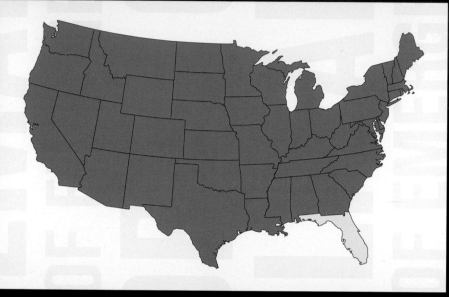

 POPULATION: 19,552,860

 SUPERCENTERS: 217

 IT'S AGAINST THE LAW TO... Fart in a public place after 6 p.m. or sell your children.

BOOTYLICIOUS

I will *not* taste the rainbow! I will never, *ever* taste that rainbow. Somebody make that rainbow stop.

WHERE'S THE BEEF?

Thanks for the sneak peek at your beef.

LET ME SEE THAT THONG

What you don't know is that the water bottle is actually filled with baby oil. You may start taking numbers on who gets to apply it.

FLORIDA

BOOOO!

Of course I'm scared...not of the ghost,
but for the fate of mankind in general.

THRICE AS NICE

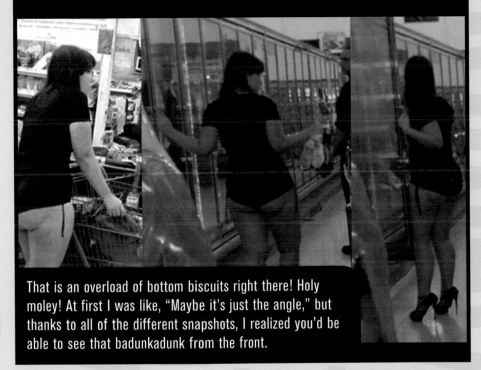

That is an overload of bottom biscuits right there! Holy moley! At first I was like, "Maybe it's just the angle," but thanks to all of the different snapshots, I realized you'd be able to see that badunkadunk from the front.

GEORGIA

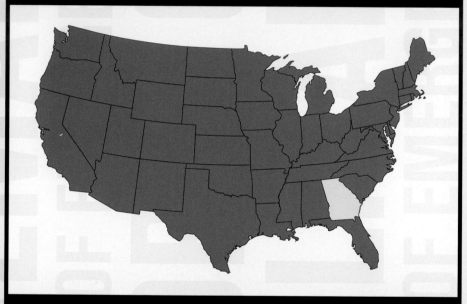

 POPULATION: 9,992,167

 SUPERCENTERS: 150

 IT'S AGAINST THE LAW TO... Eat chicken with a fork in Gainesville, the Poultry Capital of the World.

DOIN' IT DOGGY-STYLE

I'll teach you to leave me in the hot car, sweating my damn nuts off while you shop! I hope you plan on buying some paper towels and stain remover, sucker!

THE JUGS

That reminds me...I need milk.

GEORGIA

RECIPE FOR DISASTER

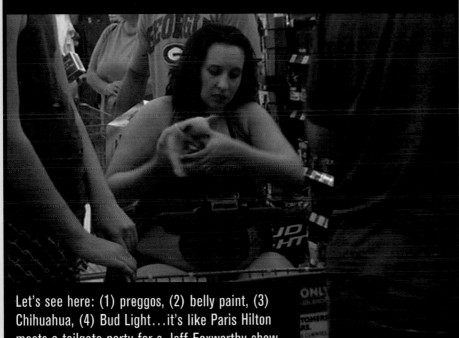

Let's see here: (1) preggos, (2) belly paint, (3) Chihuahua, (4) Bud Light...it's like Paris Hilton meets a tailgate party for a Jeff Foxworthy show.

CAPTAIN CAAAAAAVEMAAAAANNNN!

Damn girl, you are nailing that Captain Caveman look! Unga-bunga, baby!

HAWAII

 POPULATION: 1,404,054

 SUPERCENTERS: 9

 IT'S AGAINST THE LAW TO…Place a coin in one's ear.

HAWAIIAN PUNCH

Miss, just to be clear, they're remaking *Hawaii Five-O*, not Hawaii over fifty.

DOUBLE BAG IT

Here is what is so convenient about rocking plastic bags—you can shop for food and clothes in one quick swoop. Talk about killing two birds with one stone.

WHITE ON WHITE

I never thought I'd say this, but I can't wait for the summer to be over! Hurry up, Labor Day, because I'm not sure how much more see-through white clothing I can take before I lose it and jam a screwdriver into myself or someone else.

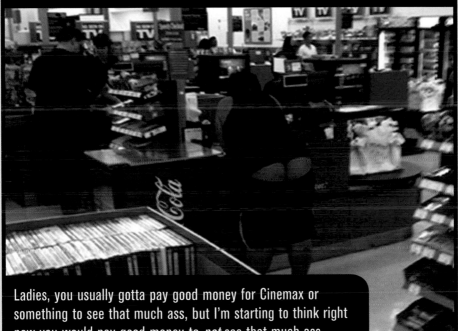

ALOHA, BRO

Ladies, you usually gotta pay good money for Cinemax or something to see that much ass, but I'm starting to think right now you would pay good money to *not* see that much ass.

IDAHO

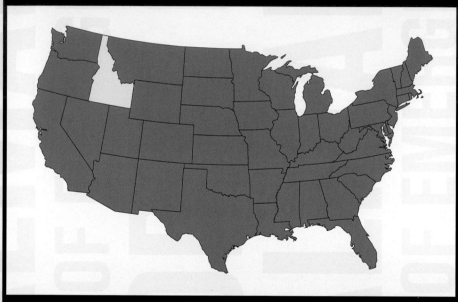

 POPULATION: 1,612,136

 SUPERCENTERS: 21

 IT'S AGAINST THE LAW TO... Fish on a camel's back.

UP IN SMOKE

I think we just found our PSA poster to prevent teen smoking!

YOU HAD A BAD DAY

Maybe now you'll think twice before you start bitching about how bad of a Monday you're having!

ILLINOIS

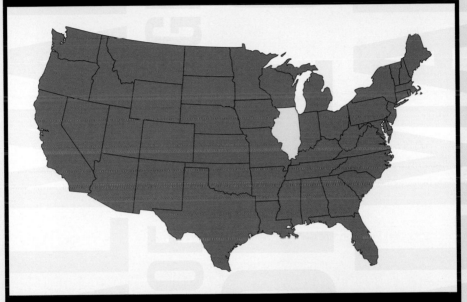

 POPULATION: 12,882,135

 SUPERCENTERS: 133

 IT'S AGAINST THE LAW TO… Have sex with a human corpse.

HEAR ME ROAR

If people mistake your gender that frequently, I would personally suggest maybe a new hairstyle or different clothing before resorting to posting a sign—or I'd tell my friends how to correctly spell "I Don't Have Balls."

ILLINOIS

OOMPA LOOMPA

That's funny, I was just wondering to myself what would happen if they had Oompa Loompas in Whoville.

THE BATHROOM BABY

At first I thought maybe she was just cool with having her kid lay on the nasty floor, but the more I think of it the more I hope this is a sweet reenactment on *I Didn't Know I Was Pregnant*.

SHEEPERS CREEPERS

Hey, Little Bo Creep, you didn't lose your sheep. They all ran away.

INDIANA

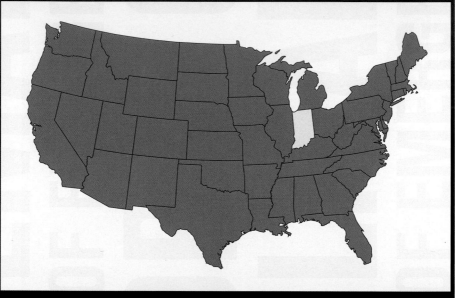

 POPULATION: 6,570,902

 SUPERCENTERS: 92

 IT'S AGAINST THE LAW TO... Take baths between the months of October and March.

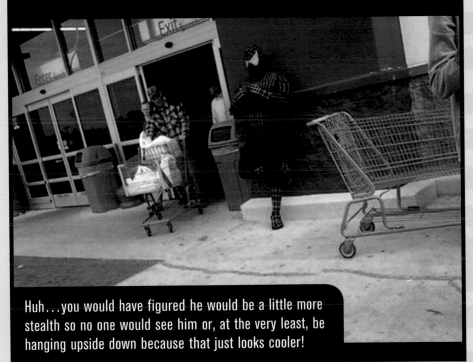

Huh...you would have figured he would be a little more stealth so no one would see him or, at the very least, be hanging upside down because that just looks cooler!

MOUNT AND DO

That, my friends, is called parking lot pimpin'! And yes, while technically she may not be a "lot lizard," I'm still pretty excited by the slop-fest that's about to go down!

MUST BE COLD

I wonder if his bra cup size is the same as his genital's cup size...

INDIANA

65

GLASS OF MILK ON A PAPER PLATE

Forget the little black cocktail dress; start rocking the tight, see-through cocktail napkin dress!

IOWA

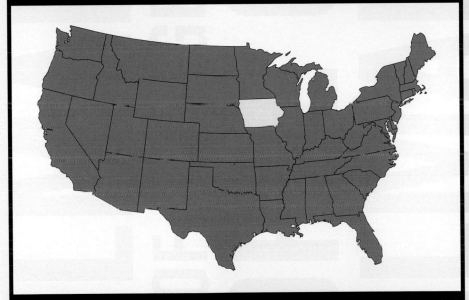

 POPULATION: 3,090,416

 SUPERCENTERS: 56

 IT'S AGAINST THE LAW TO…Use a dead person's handicapped parking sign or license plate.

THE CAT'S ASS

I think it's safe for me to assume that you drive a 1970s pedophile van and smell worse than a room full of cat sh*t.

ENCHANTMENT UNDER THE SEA

I didn't think mermaid princesses could survive that long out of water. *The Little Mermaid* was all lies!

VICTOR'S SECRET

You know what isn't one of Victoria's secrets?
That her clothing is for women.

70

ROCKIN' OUT

Ahhh yes, as the old saying goes: "Stuck between a rock and a f*cking moron!"

KANSAS

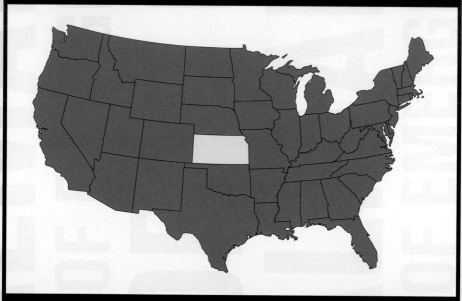

 POPULATION: 2,893,957

 SUPERCENTERS: 57

IT'S AGAINST THE LAW TO... Shoot rabbits from motorboats.

WE'RE NOT GONNA TAKE IT

This is what happens when Twisted Sister literally will not take it anymore.

GETTING SOME COLOR

I've heard of people cooking food on their car engine, but grilling pork in the parking lot? Seems gross.

KANSAS

YOGA! YOGA! YOGA!

Sexy yoga pants with boots are *not* for everybody. You don't see me rockin' skinny jeans without a shirt. I'm not David Beckham; I don't have that V muscle that goes to my crotch.

ARE YOU AFRAID?

More than you could possibly imagine. In fact,
I think I just saw Freddy Krueger piss himself.

KENTUCKY

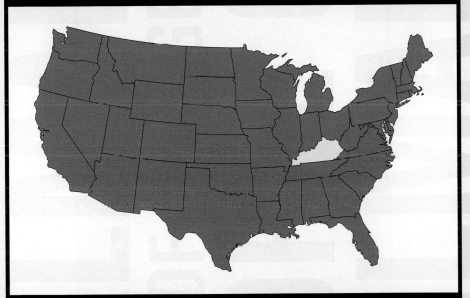

 POPULATION: 4,395,295

 SUPERCENTERS: 76

 IT'S AGAINST THE LAW TO... Dye a duckling blue and offer it for sale unless more than six are for sale at once.

CRACK THAT WHIP

I have a feeling her kids are always on their best behavior. I guess that's what happens when you have a professional spanker for a mother.

POWDERED TOAST WOMAN

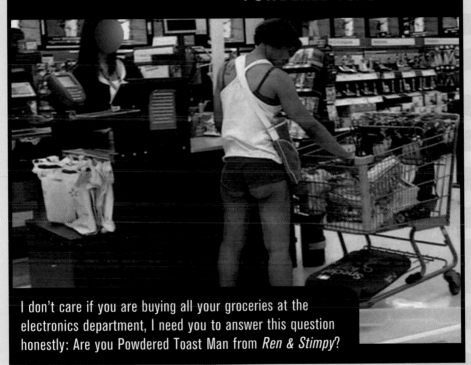

I don't care if you are buying all your groceries at the electronics department, I need you to answer this question honestly: Are you Powdered Toast Man from *Ren & Stimpy*?

MOM JORTS

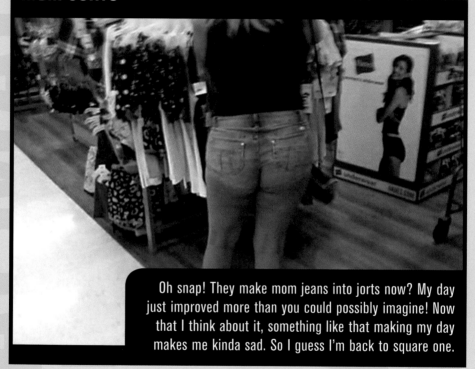

Oh snap! They make mom jeans into jorts now? My day just improved more than you could possibly imagine! Now that I think about it, something like that making my day makes me kinda sad. So I guess I'm back to square one.

COST CUTTER

Apparently he only had $5 on him...

LOUISIANA

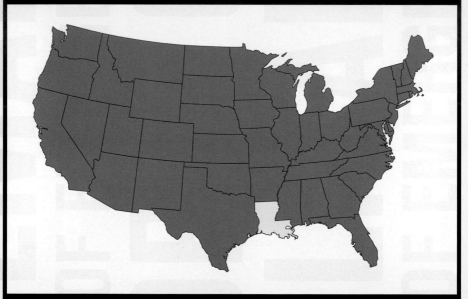

 POPULATION: 4,625,470

 SUPERCENTERS: 87

 IT'S AGAINST THE LAW TO... Instruct a pizza deliverer to deliver pizza to your friends without them knowing. The fine is $500.

HANDS BEHIND YOUR BACK

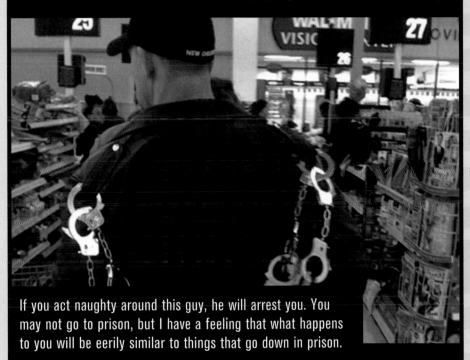

If you act naughty around this guy, he will arrest you. You may not go to prison, but I have a feeling that what happens to you will be eerily similar to things that go down in prison.

CLASS ASS

Hey, we all need someone to look up to...

LOUISIANA

THE ESCAPE FROM SHADY ACRES

Ah yes, I see you are rocking the new line of Ace Ventura tutu clothes—very nice!

GET YOUR FREAK ON

Turns out the devil does not wear Prada but Depends.

LOUISIANA

That awkward moment when your four back boobs come out and look like two hooves slipping on a ledge...

MAINE

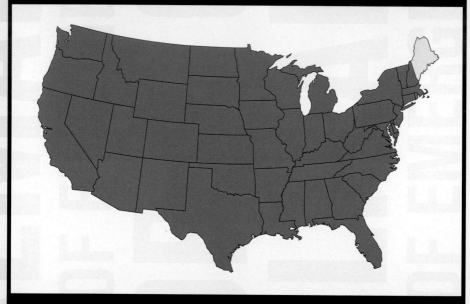

 POPULATION: 1,328,302

 SUPERCENTERS: 19

 IT'S AGAINST THE LAW TO... Have your Christmas decorations up after January 14.

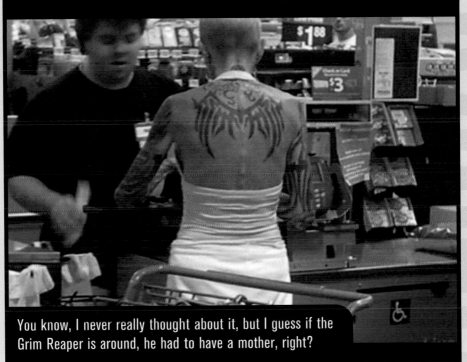

You know, I never really thought about it, but I guess if the Grim Reaper is around, he had to have a mother, right?

YELLOW MOONS

Oh, God! Had I known those were the types of yellow moons I would be getting, I never would have gone after his Lucky Charms!

MARYLAND

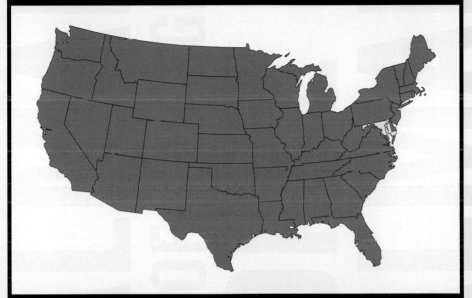

 POPULATION: 5,928,814

 SUPERCENTERS: 27

 IT'S AGAINST THE LAW TO... Take a lion to the movies in Baltimore.

KEEPIN' IT COOL

This guy knows how to keep things cool and sexy in the summer.

MARYLAND

UTI

Good luck explaining to people how you got a
urinary tract infection by washing your hands.

CHOCOLATE CAKE

I mean, if you are gonna wear some casual heels to lift and showcase your ass, you might as well showcase your ass. Am I right, or am I right?

WHO'S THE GOOSE?

When I was a kid, we played duck, duck, goose without live animals. The youth of America today are so spoiled.

MASSACHUSETTS

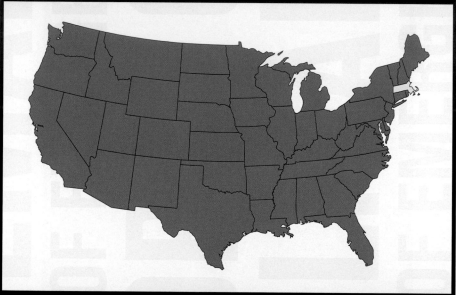

 POPULATION: 6,692,824

 SUPERCENTERS: 26

 IT'S AGAINST THE LAW TO... Purchase cigarettes if you are a child, but said child is allowed to smoke said cigarettes.

THINK TINK

Hey Tinker Bell, this isn't Neverland.
I think it's time to grow up.

MASSACHUSETTS

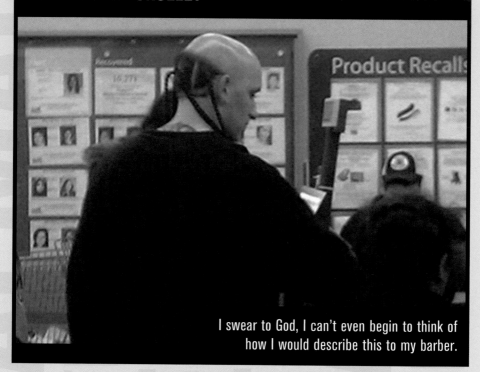

THE BRAIDED SKULLET

I swear to God, I can't even begin to think of how I would describe this to my barber.

MASSACHUSETTS

MICHIGAN

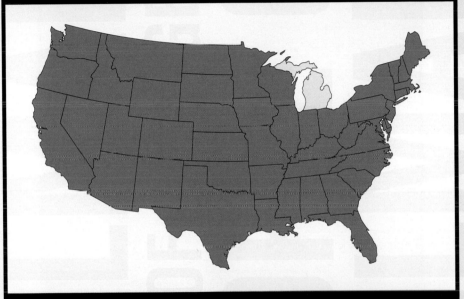

 POPULATION: 9,895,622

 SUPERCENTERS: 91

 IT'S AGAINST THE LAW TO... Cut your hair without your husband's permission if you are a woman.

NOT SO BRITE

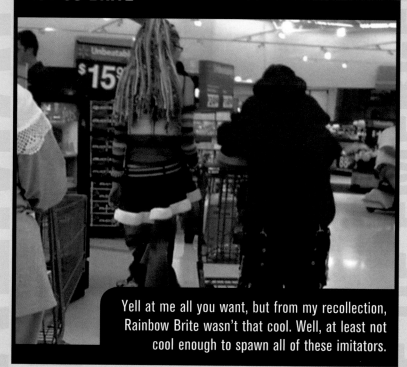

Yell at me all you want, but from my recollection, Rainbow Brite wasn't that cool. Well, at least not cool enough to spawn all of these imitators.

BOOTY JORTS

Why do your shorts looks like they are angry? If anything, we should be the ones angry at those shorts!

A WHALE OF A TAIL

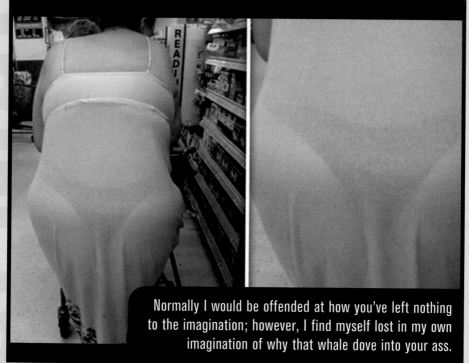

Normally I would be offended at how you've left nothing to the imagination; however, I find myself lost in my own imagination of why that whale dove into your ass.

SHE THINKS MY TRACTOR'S SEXY

That's odd...I didn't think Walmart allowed anything other than John Deere on the premises. I guess you learn something new every day!

MINNESOTA

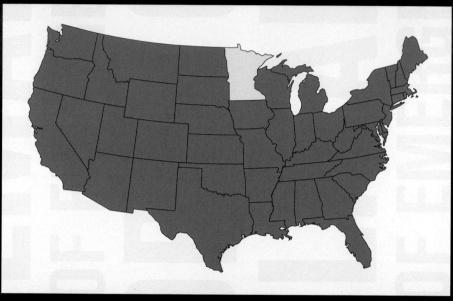

 POPULATION: 5,420,380

 SUPERCENTERS: 64

 IT'S AGAINST THE LAW TO... Cross state lines with a duck atop your head or sleep naked.

Thank God the Vikings lost, because I don't want to know what she would have worn if they made it to the Super Bowl.

A CRACK UP

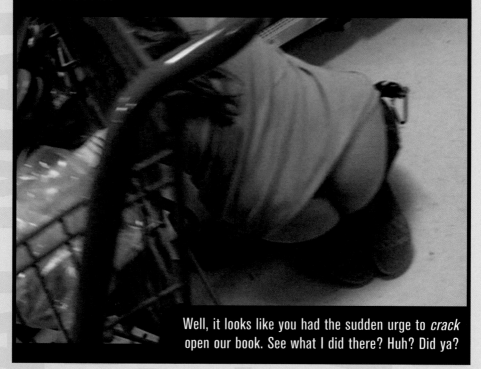

Well, it looks like you had the sudden urge to *crack* open our book. See what I did there? Huh? Did ya?

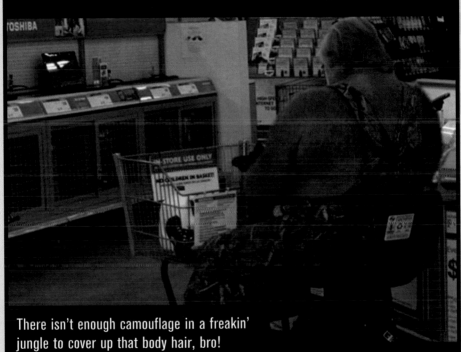

THE MIGHTY JUNGLE

There isn't enough camouflage in a freakin' jungle to cover up that body hair, bro!

YOU MIGHT BE A WALCREATURE

...if you get photographed twice in three days at your local Walmart.

MISSISSIPPI

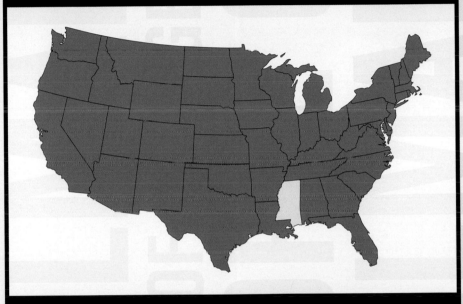

 POPULATION: 2,991,207

 SUPERCENTERS: 62

 IT'S AGAINST THE LAW TO... Voluntarily participate in unnatural intercourse; penalty is a $10,000 fine and ten-year jail sentence.

INJURY PRONE

I hope you injured that foot by kicking your own ass for wearing that out in public.

DOUBLE BUBBLE

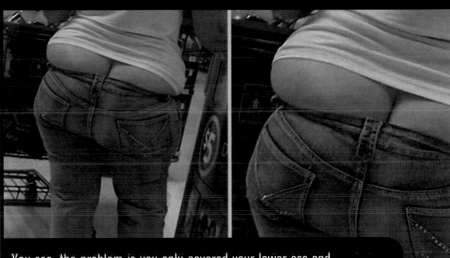

You see, the problem is you only covered your lower ass and completely ignored your upper ass. I guess I should give you the benefit of the doubt, because up until this moment I've never heard of a double butt—double chin yes, but double butt no. However, we are all now on notice, so ignorance is now no longer an excuse.

MISSISSIPPI MUD

Mississippi Mudbutts. What a good band name that would be! So to all you aspiring musicians out there looking for a name for your new rip-off Mumford and Sons band, here you go, and we expect 10 percent.

Dude, I've got some good news and some bad news. The good news (I think) is that you've got some perky titties. The bad news is they're lopsided as f*ck.

MISSOURI

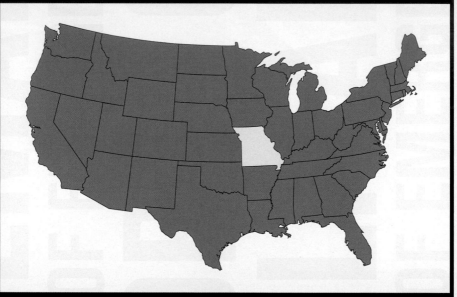

 POPULATION: 6,044,171

 SUPERCENTERS: 109

 IT'S AGAINST THE LAW TO... Buy rolling papers and tobacco in Marceline, but not lighters, if you are a minor.

AVERT YOUR EYES

Hahahahaha. I'm laughing because you can't stop looking! You don't want to, but you just can't stop! Hahahahahaha....gross.

TALK SH*T GET HIT

Ummm, quick rule of thumb: if you can fit more than two words across your ass, it's too big for you to be wearing shorts that show enough moon to turn a werewolf.

POOP, THERE IT IS

I'm not exactly sure how you got poop on the back and the side of your shorts and not the middle. I mean, my dog will roll in poop and get it there, but hopefully you have a better reason.

MONTANA

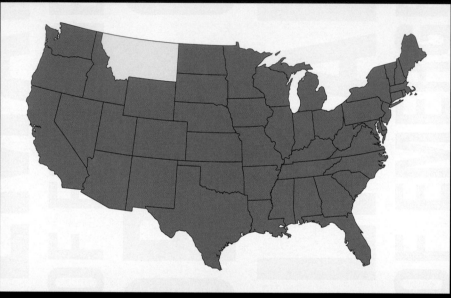

 POPULATION: 1,015,165

 SUPERCENTERS: 13

 IT'S AGAINST THE LAW TO… Have a sheep in the cab of your truck without a chaperone.

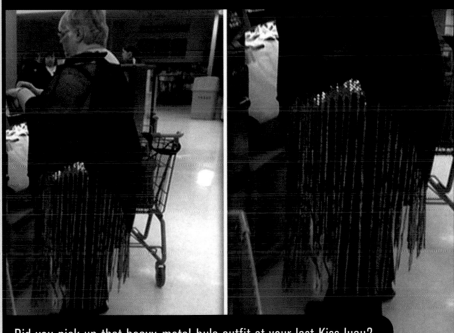

Did you pick up that heavy-metal hula outfit at your last Kiss luau?

WHO YA GONNA CALL?

I think I saw Slimer over in aisle 7. By the way, I'm the Gatekeeper. Are you the Keymaster?

THE HARVARD FASHION MAJOR

We at PoWM are not liable for any monocles broken or caviar wasted by all of you Yale alums laughing. Then again, what are the odds any Yale alums are reading our book?

SWING LOW

Ohhh, it's never a good thing when it looks like you can tuck the old boys into your hip pockets. Seriously, cleavage isn't supposed to start at your belly button.

MONTANA

NEBRASKA

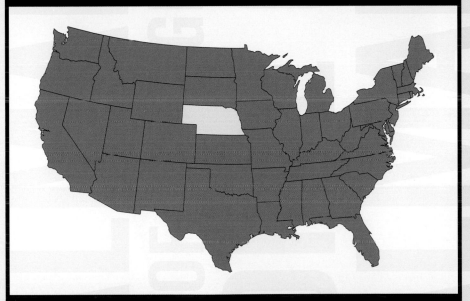

 POPULATION: 1,868,516

 SUPERCENTERS: 34

 IT'S AGAINST THE LAW TO...Get married if you have a venereal disease.

THE POOPSICLE

It looks less like you pooped your pants and more like you went down a Slip 'N Slide coated in poo.

BIG ON THE PIG

No soup or salad for this guy. He only eats ham, bacon, or any other part of the pig.

COPPIN' A SQUAT

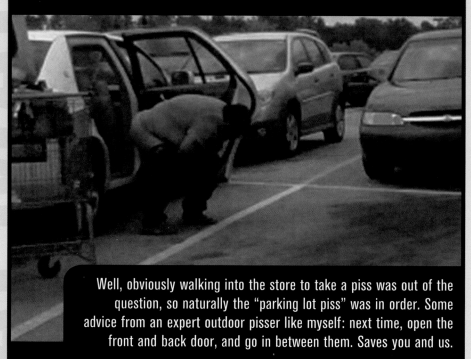

Well, obviously walking into the store to take a piss was out of the question, so naturally the "parking lot piss" was in order. Some advice from an expert outdoor pisser like myself: next time, open the front and back door, and go in between them. Saves you and us.

Duck…duck…Nope. I'm not playing this game anymore!

NEVADA

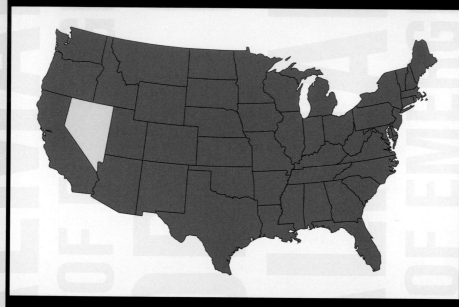

 POPULATION: 2,790,136

 SUPERCENTERS: 30

 **IT'S AGAINST THE LAW TO…**Drive a camel on the highway.

It's "bring sexy back" not "bring sexy across your whole backside."

LET IT SNOW

Wow, you severely underestimated the weather here, bub! Having a positive attitude toward the weather doesn't determine whether it will snow. Now personally, I moved south to the beach so I don't have to put up with this shit, because you gotta do more than just have Carolina on your mind to keep you and your car snow-free.

KHAKI LACKIN'

Oh, I didn't think it could get better than flesh-colored yoga pants, but apparently flesh-colored, tiny-ass khaki shorts seemed to have come along and staked it's claim to nastiest looking butt covers. What do you guys think?

GO STUPID

Ahhh OK, now I know why Big Sean says "ass" so many times. Odd how it still only barely does it justice.

NEVADA

NEW HAMPSHIRE

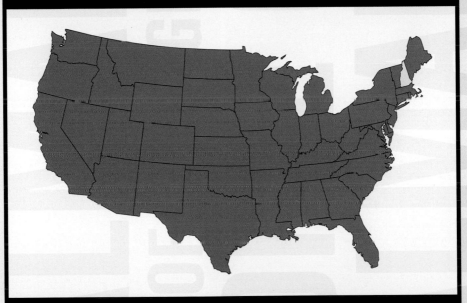

 POPULATION: 1,323,459

 SUPERCENTERS: 17

 IT'S AGAINST THE LAW TO…Relieve yourself while looking up on Sunday.

UP AND DOWN

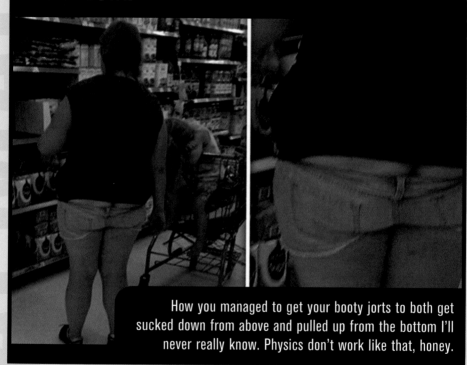

How you managed to get your booty jorts to both get sucked down from above and pulled up from the bottom I'll never really know. Physics don't work like that, honey.

NEW HAMPSHIRE

DO YOU WANT FRIES WITH THAT SHAKE?

"Shake, shake, shake. Shake, shake, shake. Shake your booty." Actually, please refrain from any further movement. My stomach couldn't possibly take any more.

NEW JERSEY

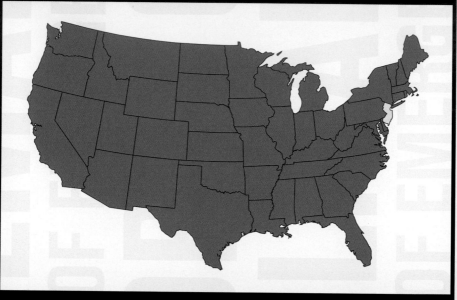

 POPULATION: 8,899,339

 SUPERCENTERS: 25

 IT'S AGAINST THE LAW TO... Knit during the fishing season if you are a man.

A LITTLE OFF THE TOP

There are more than 620,000 words in the English language and yet somehow none of them does this *any* justice.

MINTY FRESH

Judging by your shirt, I think it's safe to
assume that it's also the size of ChapStick.

I guess there is a little naughty inside all of us.

WE'RE GOING STREAKING!

For those wondering, here is an example of one of those times letting your pants hang low and not wearing a belt could come back to haunt you.

NEW MEXICO

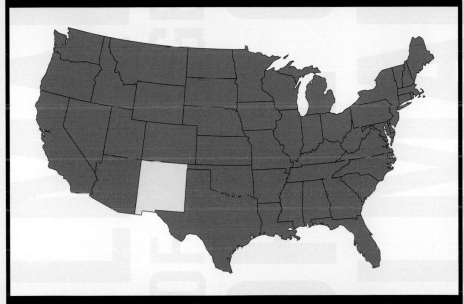

 POPULATION: 2,085,287

 SUPERCENTERS: 35

 IT'S AGAINST THE LAW TO... Have your testicles exposed if you are a man; however, other male nudity is allowed.

SYLVESTER THE CAT

Are you just making sure everyone knows they taw a puddy tat? Because I'd bet all the citizens wish Bugs Bunny and friends would have made that left at Albuquerque instead.

BOWL CUT TIMES THREE

So Mom thinks she can cut hair? Way to teach them early on that sometimes it's easier to look like a fool and give Mom what she wants rather than hear her complain, Dad!

CRACKIN' BACKS

If you step on that crack, you can be damn sure you're gonna break more than just yo mamma's back!

NEW YORK

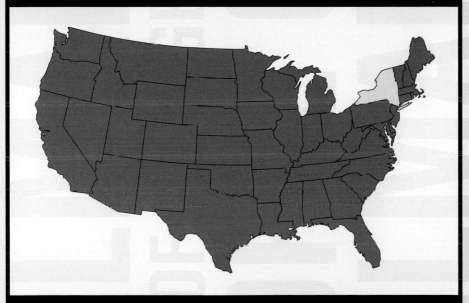

 POPULATION: 19,651,127

 SUPERCENTERS: 77

 IT'S AGAINST THE LAW TO… Greet each other by "putting one's thumb to the nose and wiggling the fingers."

ROUGHIN' IT

I don't get it. We have a trailer, a scooter, what seems to be a man taking a sh*t, shopping carts not in the cart return. I guess I'm just not looking hard enough.

NEW YORK

OK, dude, but I prefer to put my pug in a small trash can and pretend he's R2-D2. That's how I roll.

Well, I guess I shouldn't be surprised to see the "Real American" at the most American place on Earth. Whatchagonnado, brother?!

CRUELLA DE VIL: THE LATER YEARS

Listen, I don't mean to ruin the legacy of a great childhood movie, but Cruella de Vil kinda went to shit after she lost the dogs.

NORTH CAROLINA

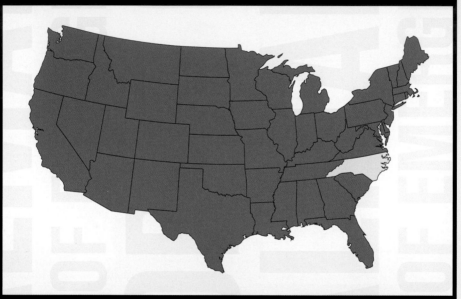

 POPULATION: 9,848,060

 SUPERCENTERS: 139

 IT'S AGAINST THE LAW TO… Use elephants to plow cotton fields.

SHOCK VALUE

Thanks for letting us all "Marvel" at you, real-life Storm. Maybe some day we will all be fortunate enough to find out your powers ran out and you electrocuted yourself.

NESTLE CHUNKY

Remember how when you were growing up you always thought having X-ray vision would be the greatest thing in the world? Yeah, I'll let you stew on that for a while and reconsider your friend's argument for being able to fly as the best power.

SAND BAGGIN'

And the award for longest cleavage goes to...Seriously, though, boobs are supposed to stick out. So if you can pull your shirt down to your knees and still not flash anyone, how 'bout we cover up those deflated balloons and just go back to yearning for the good ol' days when they had some perk.

THE PRICE OF SILVER

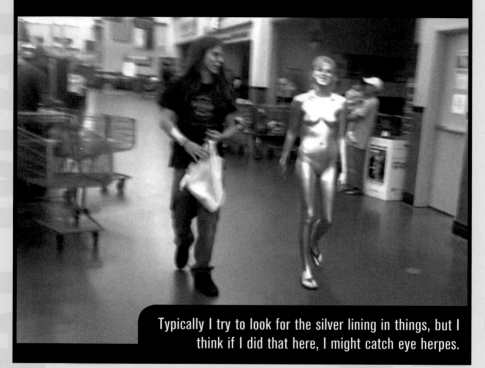

Typically I try to look for the silver lining in things, but I
think if I did that here, I might catch eye herpes.

NORTH CAROLINA

CHOKING HAZARD

It's ironic, because they had to put a bag over your mother's head to make you...and *boom* goes the dynamite!

NORTH CAROLINA

NORTH DAKOTA

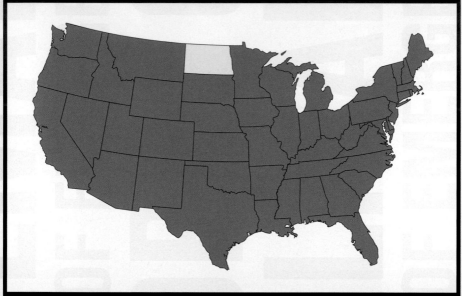

 POPULATION: 723,393

 SUPERCENTERS: 14

 IT'S AGAINST THE LAW TO... Serve beer and pretzels at the same time in any bar or restaurant.

I WORK OUT

Mmmmm, don't you just love the smell of beer gut in the morning?!

WHISKERS, CUPCAKE, AND SPRINKLES

In case anyone else was out there wondering what they could get tattooed on their body to let the world know they are sad and lonely, the answer is cats.

OHIO

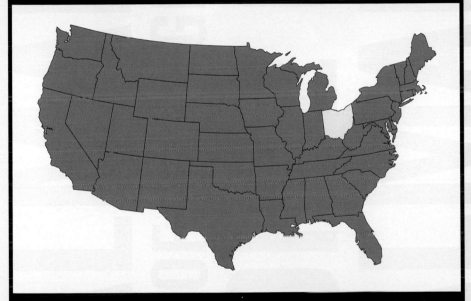

 POPULATION: 11,570,808

 SUPERCENTERS: 139

 IT'S AGAINST THE LAW TO… Get a fish drunk.

IT'S SO FLUFFY!

Oh, if those unicorns could talk...to someone other than the group of stuffed animals he performs for in his basement.

OHIO

BLACK-ON-BLACK CRIME

Of course the tank top has to be see-through mesh. How else could you see his thong sticking out of his short shorts?

SHE LIKES TO PARTY

Oh snap! I see you are trying to pull off the "party in the front, party in the back" mullet...Fortune favors the bold.

OHIO

SCUBA STEVE, DAMN YOU!

"How ya doin'? I'm Scuba Sam, Scuba Steve's father. You see, my boy needs to take a bath—the only problem is he's afraid to bathe alone. So, I was wondering if you'd keep him company in the tub. Terrific, and after your bath, you need to try and study hard, because if you want to be in the Scuba Squad, you have to be smart."

OKLAHOMA

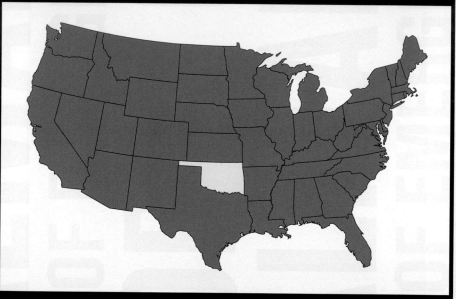

 POPULATION: 3,850,568

 SUPERCENTERS: 79

 IT'S AGAINST THE LAW TO... Have sex with a buffalo inside a bar.

RAINBOW BILL

Oh damn! Mr. Skittles must be getting jealous of all the attention Willy the Pimp gets.

BREAK A LEG

I guess that's a little more subtle than "I want you to sit on my face." Good luck with that, bro.

OKLAHOMA

BURNIN' LOVE

If your first thought is anything other than slapping her back hard enough to cause injury to your own hand, then feel free to close this book, because you are not the type of fans we have come to know and love around here.

BLOWN COVERAGE

Listen, lady, I doubt the Pacific tsunami is gonna make it's way to your local Walmart in Oklahoma.

OKLAHOMA

OREGON

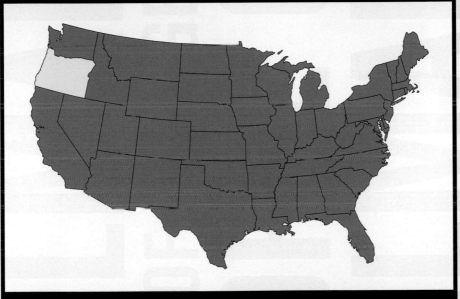

 POPULATION: 3,930,065

 SUPERCENTERS: 28

 IT'S AGAINST THE LAW TO... Place a container filled with human fecal matter on the side of any highway.

BOOTY TALK

Oh, OK. I was just going to ask where you got those cute boots.

MARIO KART

Awww, that's heartbreaking. Mario is reminiscing about the good ol' days when he only had to jump over turtles and collect coins. Now Nintendo's got him doing all sorts of crazy stuff, and it's starting to take a toll on the old guy.

FRESH VEGGIES

There have been double-digit instances of children with bags on their heads at Walmart, and we've got the photographic evidence to prove it. You would figure one would be enough for the few who didn't know this was a bad idea to actually learn that it was. "Here, little Johnny, play with this noose—I've got to pick out tonight's dinner."

'TIL DOUGHNUTS DO US PART

I now pronounce you lazy and settling.

AUNT LIZA

Because being the crazy cat lady is so 2008.

OREGON

PENNSYLVANIA

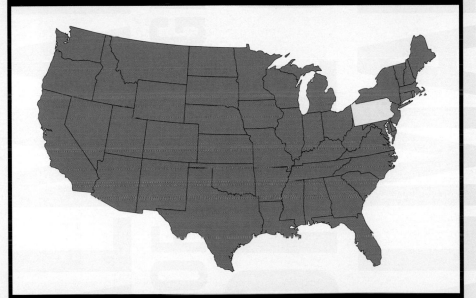

 POPULATION: 12,773,801

 SUPERCENTERS: 114

 IT'S AGAINST THE LAW TO...Sleep on top of a refrigerator outdoors.

AGONY OF DA FEET

Here is a list of things worth fighting someone over at Walmart: (1)...sorry, I couldn't think of anything.

I GOTTA PEE

Hmmmmm, well, we don't like to make fun of people with medical problems, but I have no problem making fun of someone with a medical problem who is inconsiderate enough to gross me out. Tell you what, I'll continue to be sympathetic to your issues, but how 'bout you be sympathetic to the fact that I don't want to see your piss bag while I'm picking up some deli meat?!

LAYED OUT

Did he drink too much and pass out? Did he see someone from our site and pass out? Either way, what I want to hear is the conversation between the two cops...

COWABUNGA!

Probably picking up some pizzas! TMNT brings me back to the good ol' days.

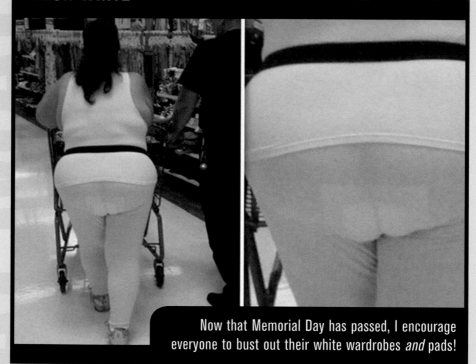

FRESH WHITE

Now that Memorial Day has passed, I encourage everyone to bust out their white wardrobes *and* pads!

RHODE ISLAND

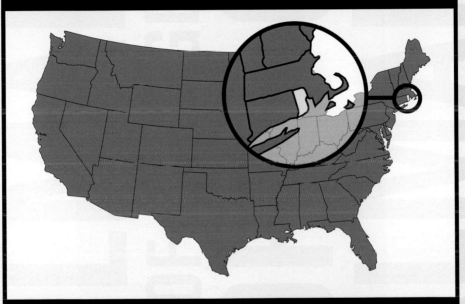

 POPULATION: 1,051,511

 SUPERCENTERS: 5

 IT'S AGAINST THE LAW TO... Bite off another person's leg or throw pickle juice on a trolley.

OOPS, I CRAPPED MY PANTS

Inconvenient: shitting your pants. Convenient: shitting your pants at Walmart where they sell replacement pants! That is the definition of wrong time, right place.

BIRD IS THE WORD

Maybe someone should make birdcages bigger.
I don't need some giant parrot squawking at
me and shitting all over the floor while I shop.

SOUTH CAROLINA

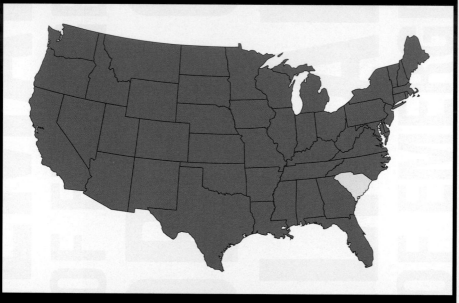

 POPULATION: 4,774,839

 SUPERCENTERS: 80

 IT'S AGAINST THE LAW TO... Play a pinball machine if you are under eighteen years of age.

I guess Chester Cheetah needs a disguise when he goes out in public. Makes sense; you don't want people bothering you for autographs and free Cheetos. Although I think he needs to work on his disguise just a bit.

WELL, HELLO THERE!

I feel like it's smiling at me and I can't stop smiling back like a goofy idiot.

SOUTH CAROLINA

FOR $50, I'LL RIP IT OFF

Honey, if you have to ask, you can't afford it.

SOUTH CAROLINA

187

BIKER BABES

This picture is near and dear to my heart because the PoWM headquarters are in the fine town of Myrtle Beach, South Carolina, and I know all too well about Black Bike Week, which is basically a parade of PoWM—And. It. Is. *Glorious!* We never miss a chance to people watch.

SOUTH DAKOTA

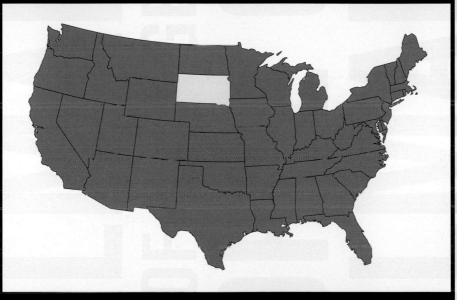

 POPULATION: 844,877

 SUPERCENTERS: 14

 IT'S AGAINST THE LAW TO... Lie down and fall asleep in a cheese factory.

TOP SHELF

It really makes you wonder what goes onto that shelf.

SOUTH DAKOTA

TESTING HIS BOOB PRESSURE

Why roll up your sleeves? Another way to check your blood pressure is by clamping the testing device on your left nipple. See, you learn something new every day.

PHOTO HUNT

SOUTH DAKOTA

OK folks, we're gonna have ourselves a little image search a la *Highlights* magazine. Please check off as you go:

- ☐ Lay's Staxs (a.k.a. bullshit Pringles)
- ☐ A watermelon
- ☐ Beneful dog food (that's what I give my dog because she is awesome)
- ☐ Total cereal
- ☐ A baby
- ☐ Yoplait Light yogurt
- ☐ Frozen peas

Before everyone starts judging her and condemning her, please remember that it's OK because some people actually *like* the taste of light yogurt. That's what you guys were pissed and shocked about, right?

TENNESSEE

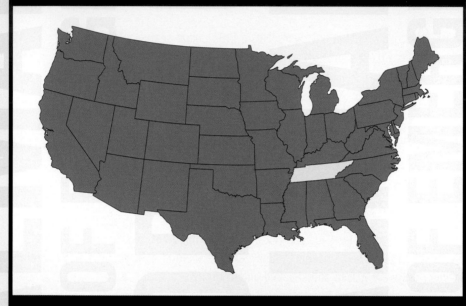

 POPULATION: 6,495,978

 SUPERCENTERS: 112

 IT'S AGAINST THE LAW TO…Share your Netflix password.

MOULIN ROUGE

The real Lady Marmalade...not the
sexy version, the fruit preserve.

SNOOKI WANT SMUSH-SMUSH

Hey, Snooki, thanks for the effort you put into covering up. That's probably the same type of effort that got you booted from community college.

THE COOKIE MONSTER

WHO THE F*CK BAKES
COOKIES IN THEIR CAR?

TENNESSEE

THE CEREAL KILLER

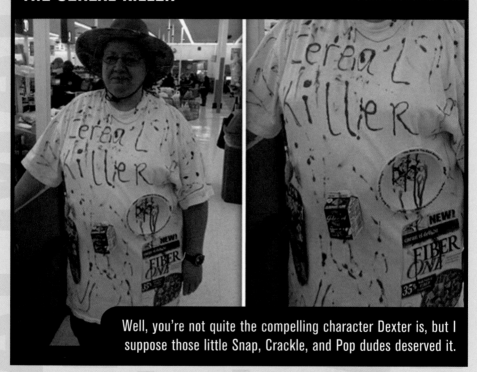

Well, you're not quite the compelling character Dexter is, but I suppose those little Snap, Crackle, and Pop dudes deserved it.

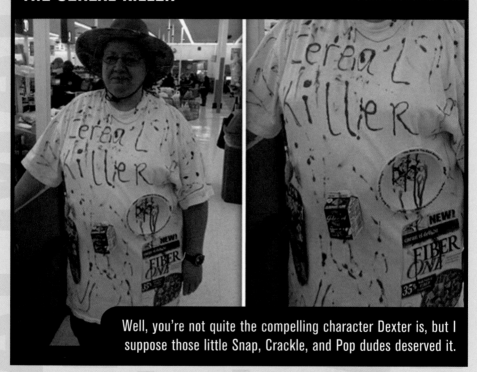

TEXAS

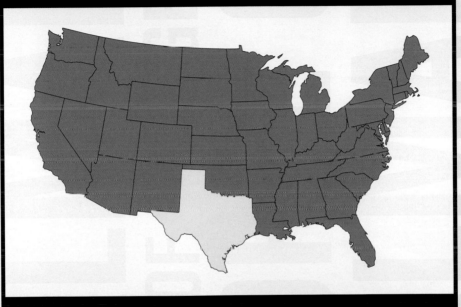

 POPULATION: 26,448,193

 SUPERCENTERS: 361

 IT'S AGAINST THE LAW TO... Take more than three sips of beer at a time while standing.

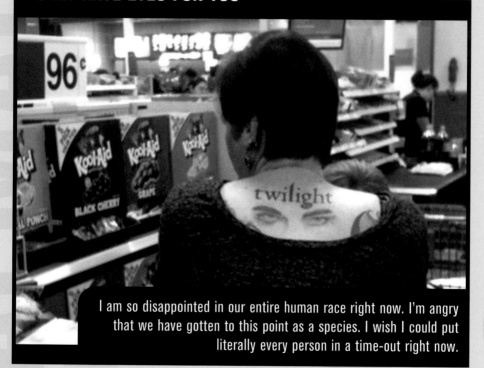

I ONLY HAVE EYES FOR YOU

I am so disappointed in our entire human race right now. I'm angry that we have gotten to this point as a species. I wish I could put literally every person in a time-out right now.

Hey, Maria Sharapova, how 'bout we leave the tennis outfits to the pros?

SHEEPISH BEHAVIOR

Anywhere else in the world it would probably be weird to say you saw a sheep in a diaper. Your friends would probably call bullshit. But say you saw it in a Walmart parking lot—boom, instant credibility.

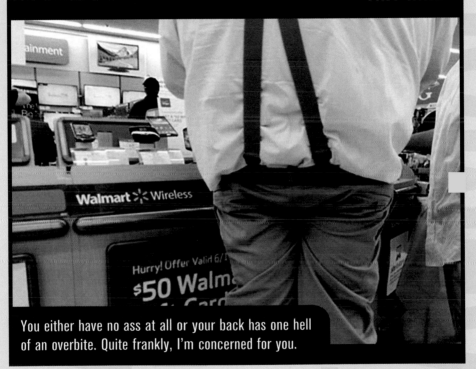

TINY HINEY

You either have no ass at all or your back has one hell of an overbite. Quite frankly, I'm concerned for you.

ROUNDING SECOND

I think you can get to second base just by giving her a hug.

TEXAS

THE BUTTERSCOTCH CHIP

Hershey's has a new butterscotch chip! Now, somebody go get us a few barrels of cookie dough.

UTAH

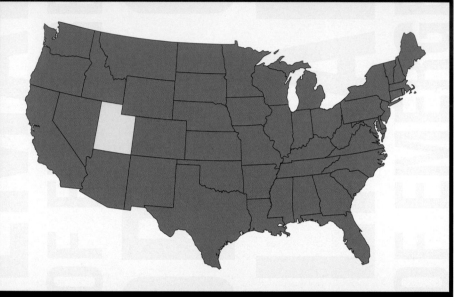

 POPULATION: 2,900,872

 SUPERCENTERS: 40

 IT'S AGAINST THE LAW TO... Have sex in the back of an ambulance if it is responding to an emergency call.

ONE WISE MAN

Even the Three Wise Men do their Christmas and birthday shopping at Walmart. I wonder if he was able to get that ZhuZhu Pet for baby Jesus.

UTAH

BREAST WISHES

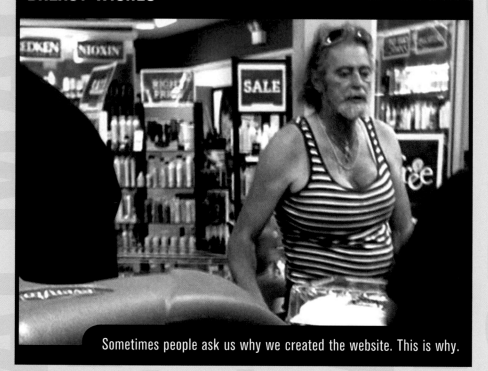

Sometimes people ask us why we created the website. This is why.

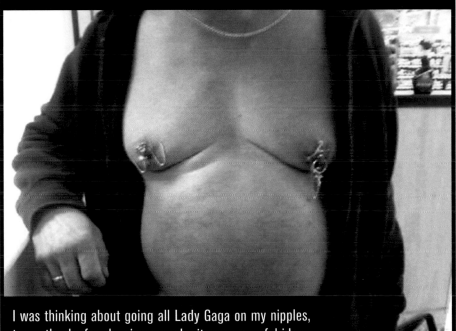

I was thinking about going all Lady Gaga on my nipples, too…thanks for showing me why it was an awful idea.

THE BROWN BUTTERFLY

I call these sharts "The Butterfly Effect" because when you bend over, it looks like you sat on a butterfly.

VERMONT

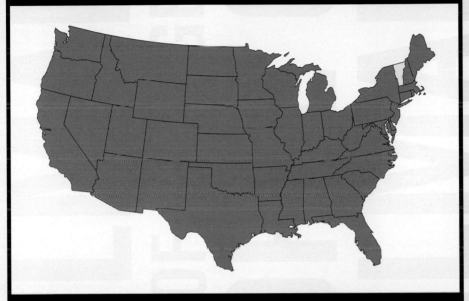

 POPULATION: 626,630

 SUPERCENTERS: 1

 IT'S AGAINST THE LAW TO... Wear false teeth without your husband's permission if you are a woman.

GOBBLE, GOBBLE

Can't decide who's got it worse in this picture: the stuffed turkey crammed on his head or the stuffing he's going cram in his mouth later.

THE PICKUP ARTIST

Nothing like pickin' up chicks in the snacks aisle on a Friday night. They're so lonely it's like shooting fish in a barrel.

VIRGINIA

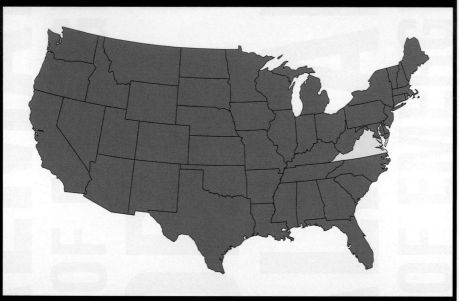

 POPULATION: 8,260,405

 SUPERCENTERS: 104

 IT'S AGAINST THE LAW TO...Have oral or anal sex.

"Hey, PoWM, how do you know if someone has too much time on their hands?" Great question. Well, a terrific start would be to spot the person who created his own moronic shirt to distract people from the absolutely awful mess he created on his head.

GUT CHECK

Oh, good, I was getting sick of seeing ass cracks. I'm glad you decided to instead show us all your gut crack. It's a pleasant change of scenery.

I'M SUPER, THANKS FOR ASKING

Oh snap! Look at him/her workin' it! I gotta be honest. Once I saw this, I couldn't take my eyes off those legs...uhhh, I mean that goatee.

PICK YOUR POISON

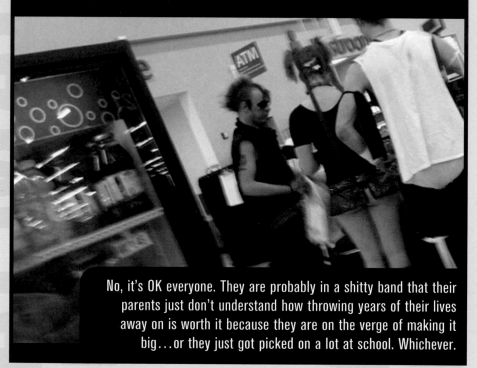

No, it's OK everyone. They are probably in a shitty band that their parents just don't understand how throwing years of their lives away on is worth it because they are on the verge of making it big…or they just got picked on a lot at school. Whichever.

WASHINGTON

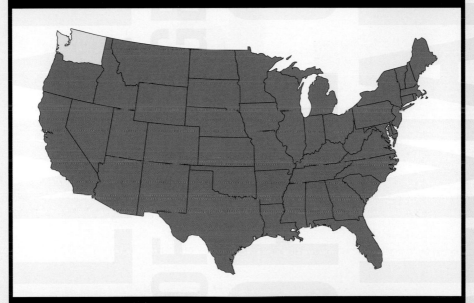

 POPULATION: 6,971,406

 SUPERCENTERS: 50

 IT'S AGAINST THE LAW TO... Harass Bigfoot, Sasquatch, or other undiscovered subspecies. Doing so is a felony.

WASHINGTON IS NICE THIS TIME OF YEAR

Did you wear that so you could swim in my tears?

She likes to check out in the express lane—the Panda Express. Problem is, her cart is empty again an hour later.

FUN BAGS

Those bags you're carrying seem extremely heavy and hard to lug around. The ones in your hand look full and hard to keep up, too!

WOOKIE WHAT WE HAVE HERE

I present to you the queen of the Wookies in all her glory! No other words need to be said, other than that she is weavetastic, which isn't even a word, so technically I was right: no other words needed to be said.

WEST VIRGINIA

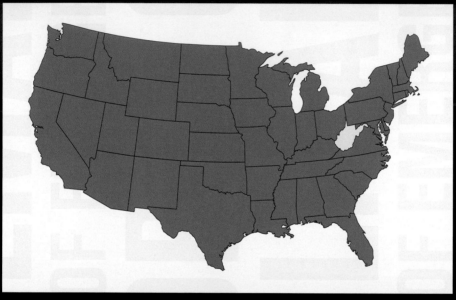

 POPULATION: 1,854,304

 SUPERCENTERS: 38

 IT'S AGAINST THE LAW TO… Have sex with an animal if it exceeds forty pounds.

HAM 'N CHEESE

Someone grab me a knife and bread, I'm 'bout to carve me up a ham sammich!

AMERICA, F*CK YEAH!

What's more American than Daisy Dukes and a U.S. flag bikini top? Bigger Daisy Dukes and U.S. flag bikini, duh! Go America!

MY HEART SKIPS A BEAT

Well, that's fitting, because she definitely stole my heart…what's that?
Oh, I'm having a heart attack? OK, yeah, that makes more sense.

AN EXTRA LIFE

The good news is your ass looks like the 1-Up from Super Mario. The bad news is if that's what I have to touch to get that extra life, I don't think it's worth it.

WISCONSIN

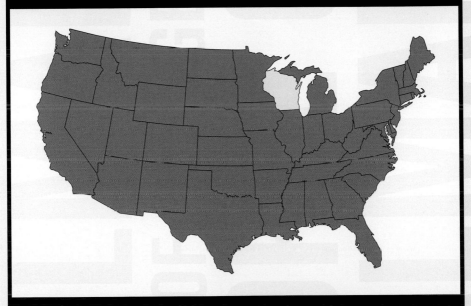

 POPULATION: 5,742,713

 SUPERCENTERS: 80

 IT'S AGAINST THE LAW TO... Serve apple pie in public restaurants without cheese.

LET ME TAIL YOU SOMETHING

Let me tell you a tail tale of a man who still couldn't keep his pants up even with that extra support back there.

WALMART'S BELIEVE IT OR NOT

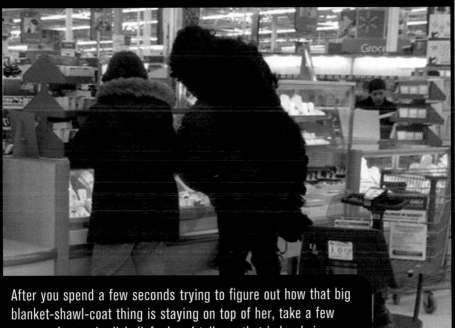

After you spend a few seconds trying to figure out how that big blanket-shawl-coat thing is staying on top of her, take a few more and stare in disbelief when I tell you that is her hair.

HOT DIGGITY DOGGLES

Doggles: because his dog is cooler than yours.

WISCONSIN

WYOMING

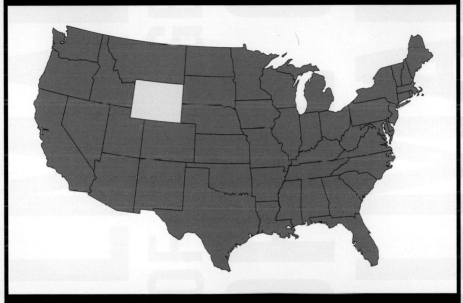

  POPULATION: 582,658

SUPERCENTERS: 10

 IT'S AGAINST THE LAW TO… Wear a hat that obstructs people's view in a public theater or place of amusement.

THAT B, DOUBLE O, T, Y

Sometimes yoga pants are worn for our viewing pleasure, sometimes for comfort, sometimes for actual yoga, but here I think the purpose is ventilation. I just don't see it falling into any of the other categories.

SOMEWHERE SISQO IS CRYING

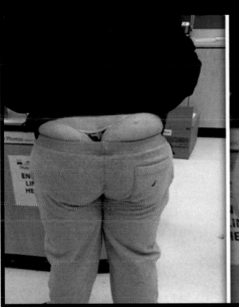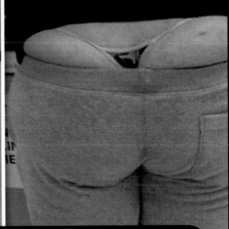

It's easier for me to imagine a tiny person using that thong as a parachute to glide down your crack than you actually wearing that on purpose.

HERE COMES THE BOOM

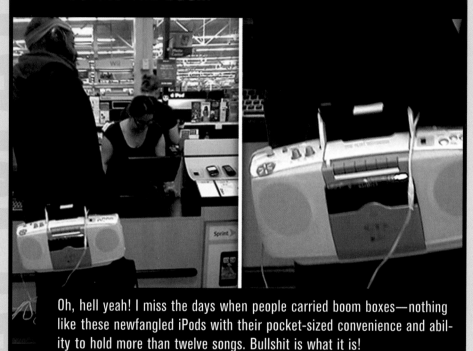

Oh, hell yeah! I miss the days when people carried boom boxes—nothing like these newfangled iPods with their pocket-sized convenience and ability to hold more than twelve songs. Bullshit is what it is!

PASSPORT

The United States isn't the only country to house Walmarts and their inhabitants! Check out some other offerings from Canada, Mexico, and Puerto Rico, where Walmartians also congregate!

CANADA

POPULATION: 35,540,400

SUPERCENTERS: 259

IT'S AGAINST THE LAW TO... Make burgers out of polar bears.

STOP LISTENING TO HIM

CAUSE STONE COLD SAID SO.

I don't think your hamburger is the only thing you need help with.

CANADA

DAT BOOTY THO

Even bottom biscuits cooked to perfection are inappropriate...I think. Actually I'm not sure about that at all. I'm starting to think that's absolutely fine. But I should stick to my guns and say no, right? Maybe? I don't know. But consider the children, right? Well, kids forget stuff, so yes? My mind is at war and I'm scared.

MEXICO

 POPULATION: 123,278,559

 SUPERCENTERS: 244

IT'S AGAINST THE LAW TO... Say to anyone, "Have a nice day."

I SAW MOMMY HUMPING SANTA CLAUS

Well, this just has me wondering what's being stuffed in the stockings…a yule log, perhaps?

TASTE THE BEAST MODE

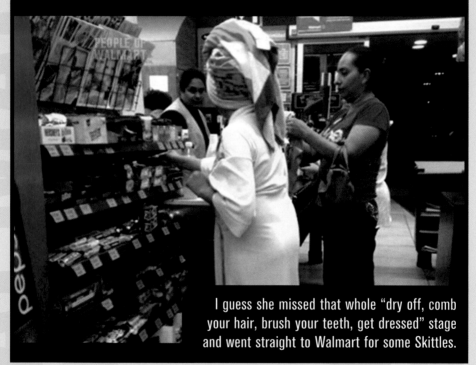

I guess she missed that whole "dry off, comb your hair, brush your teeth, get dressed" stage and went straight to Walmart for some Skittles.

PUERTO RICO

 POPULATION: 3,615,086

 SUPERCENTERS: 12

 IT'S AGAINST THE LAW TO... Buy bread after 5 p.m. on Sundays.

STICK UP

This, I believe, is our first submission from the great U.S. territory of Puerto Rico! That being said, I have no idea whether colorful Popsicle-stick hats are common down there but I'm gonna go out on a limb and say not so much. If they are, let's just be happy they can't vote.

THE BAKED POTATO

♫ I see you got your baked potato and your flippy floppies, walkin' around Walmart looking all sorts of sloppy. ♫

PUERTO RICO

SOURCES

1. U.S. Census Bureau, "Annual Estimates of the Population for the United States, Regions, States, and Puerto Rico: April 1, 2010 to July 1, 2013 (NST-EST2013-01)," Population Estimates, State Totals: Vintage 2013, table 1, accessed April 2014, http://www.census.gov/popest/data/state/totals/2013/index.html.

2. Walmart Corporation. "Our Locations," Interactive Map, accessed October 23, 2014, http://corporate.walmart.com/our-story/our-business/locations/.

3. Government of Canada, "Canada's Population Estimates: Age and Sex, 2014," Statistics Canada, last modified September 26, 2014, http://www.statcan.gc.ca/daily-quotidien/140926/dq140926b-eng.htm?HPA.

4. "Dumb Laws." www.dumblaws.com.

5. World Population Statistics, "Population of Mexico 2014," last modified March 20, 2014, www.worldpopulationstatistics.com/population-of-mexico-2014/.

ABOUT THE AUTHORS

Adam Kipple, Andrew Kipple, and Luke Wherry all grew up in the same town of Harrison City, Pennsylvania, located just outside of Pittsburgh. Adam (thirty) is a web designer who graduated from the Art Institute of Pittsburgh and currently resides in Myrtle Beach, South Carolina, along with Luke (twenty-eight), a graduate of University of Pittsburgh, and Andrew (twenty-eight) a graduate of Xavier University and Valparaiso University School of Law. More recently, the trio expanded their website properties into the humor blog network Three Ring Blogs, which now has more than twenty-five hilarious websites. They also opened their web design and marketing company, Three Ring Focus.

Adam and his wife, Breann, welcomed their badass son Jackson to the world, and Luke and his wife, Mindy, are enjoying their beautiful daughter Madison a.k.a. Princess Puffy Cheeks. Andrew is still a sad, lonely man with nothing to carry on his legacy besides dirty butt cracks and side boobs.